Praise for *Playing Chicken with an Iron Horse*

Ginsberg, Hughes, and Wolff move over! Fred Rosenblum's latest poetry collection, *Playing Chicken with an Iron Horse*, follows a boy's misadventures and tomfooleries while "corn stalking the minefields of juvenile tragedy." Engaged in Chinese checkers, mumbly peg and discovering girls don't have penises, the boy matures and much later joins the Marines "to keep our country safe from the commies" but still "laughing about the stupidest shit." For those who've nearly reached the exit ramp of life, Rosenblum's poetry brings "crafted echoes" from a place so close to our own, we feel the splinters he describes as the "tickling torture" in the back of a '53 GMC flatbed.
—Kate Porter, author of *Lessons in Disguise*

This book is a gritty time machine into 1950s and 60s El Cajon, San Diego, Los Angeles, where urchins pelt a "little red Austin Healey" with loquats, panic at a floating turd in De Anza Cove, suffer a father's practical joke in "The Hotel Cecil," toss revenge eggs at houses and school, and relish in mostly hidden sexual energy. Dirt clod fights in "eucalypti / & groves of pepper and oak / [. . .] bulldozed-over / by the murderous machinery of time" come alive in these pages. "Ice Cream Bandits" innocence is lost when El Cajon police leave "handcuffed, bone-bruised wrists" to be rubbed by a father's salve. These honest, bold, revealing poems delight in scenes of teen mischief before initiation in "the farcical war in Southeast Asia."
— Scott T. Starbuck, author of *Carbonfish Blues, Hawk on Wire*, and *Industrial Oz*

Playing Chicken with an Iron Horse evokes the vivid image of a mischievous, blue-collar childhood from the '50s and '60s, recapturing the reckless abandon of adolescence while simultaneously alluding to the future loss of America's mid-century ethos, over the horizon and across the ocean in Vietnam. Rosenblum laments this passing free spirit of youth via the free-style, hybridized verse he employs — a requiem for innocence.
— Katt Blackwell-Starnes, Educator, Lamar University

My wife and I play a little game when an author is being interviewed on the radio about his or her working class background. Will the author say at some point ... and then I went to Harvard? If not Harvard another elite college. Very few fail to do so. It gives us a good laugh. Fred's college was the U.S. Marine Corps followed by graduate study in Vietnam. His background is working class, and his poems reflect that vanishing world. They will make you laugh and cry. Fred is, as young people say, authentic.
— Tom Sexton, former Poet Laureate of Alaska, whose latest collection is entitled *Li Bai Rides a Celestial Dolphin Home*

Playing Chicken
with an
Iron Horse

Also by Fred Rosenblum

Hollow Tin Jingles

Vietnumb

Playing Chicken with an Iron Horse

Fred Rosenblum

Fomite
Burlington, VT

Copyright © 2019 Fred Rosenblum
Cover image - Photo by bantersnaps on Unsplash

All rights reserved. No part of this book may be reproduced in any form or by any means without the prior written consent of the publisher, except in the case of brief quotations used in reviews and certain other noncommercial uses permitted by copyright law.

ISBN-978-1-947917-29-3
Library of Congress Control Number: 2019945990

Fomite
58 Peru Street
Burlington, VT 05401
www.fomitepress.com

In memory of the songbirds: Mom, Dad, Gerry and Grandma Beulah

Thanks goes out to the following who thought enough of my poems to make them public:

Cholla Needles, Main Street Rag, Neologism Poetry Journal, Pif Magazine, Pudding Magazine

Contents

Preface —	1
No '... Indians Scattered on Dawn's Highway Bleeding ...'	3
M. I. C., See You Real Soon…	4
The Grigsby Kid	6
De Anza Cove	7
The Hotel Cecil	10
Feigning Innocence	12
Brownie	13
The Wailing of Cats	14
Number One Seed	18
Tumescent Pleasures	20
Janie	22
Black Sheep	24
Free Drinks	25
Killing Time	26
Pigeonholed	28
Grey Cedar Farmhouse Weekend Sleepover	29
Long Before I Knew the Rifleman Was a Dodger	34
Happy Birthday Sir, September 12, 1957	36
El Cajon Valley	38
A Mitzvah	39
The Dressing Room	41
Riverwalk	43
Cajon Speedway	44
… That I Would Cheat That Poor Old Woman	45
Mid-Century Sketch	48
Sadie Hawkins Dance	51
Dead Comedians	53
Sort of a Robin Hoodlum	55
Dinger	56
Half Day Boat, Shelter Island	57
Day of Darkness	59
Ice Cream Bandits	61

Cathedral Hills	62
Pool Guests	64
Spit Pea Soup	65
On the Cusp of the Hep Cats and the Hippies	66
Conquering Cock Rock	67
Resigning Myself to the Dotted Line	69
Truant Officer	70
Afterthoughts —	75
About the Author	79

Preface —

The following sketches of my youth span 18 years — beginning in St. Louis, MO in '49 and ending with my recruitment into the military service in '67. In 1954, we sang two thousand miles of patriotic ditties, Christian hymns, and Crosby hits, an incongruous medley, considering our route through the Cheyenne, Navajo, and Hopi nations — songs that occupied us during our recessions of hamburger and hot cake sustenance. With our dry throats croaking, the five of us: my parents, my grandmother, brother and me, self-proclaimed, *Sour Notes* — off key, but pioneering spirits, pressed forward in perfect disharmony, all the way out west to California — in search of The American Dream, or some such.

Today, I'm the lone survivor of that raucous, crooning quintet, and before I rejoin those old songbirds, I've vowed to share these recollections; that I might recapture a modicum of the pulse of my generation, deluge of post-World War II progeny, and otherwise regenerative stock, also known as, "Baby Boomers." This collection serves as a mere scintilla of the thanks I feel — a tribute to this magical gift of existence.

Save for the first few pieces, the bulk of what remains, draws on anecdotes and/or episodes from '58 to '67, during which time, my parents purchased a three bedroom tract home for 15 thousand dollars (for what one might pay upwards of 400 K today), in East San Diego County. El Cajon was a sparsely populated suburb of San Diego – a sprawling, quiet little farming community of Caucasian, Mexican, and Native American families, nestled into pockets of brushy, undulating foothills, and granite mountains. A vision of expansion in the mid-1950's, El Cajon wouldn't realize optimum clarity for twenty-five years, its actual evolution entirely unforeseen. At present, over-population, homelessness, and the educationally-challenged, have completely undermined its conception. Out of squalor and ignorance, a prevailing flux of drugs and crime, runs rampant through the streets of "The Box" today – a sad pallor on my fond recollection of youth.

No '... Indians Scattered on Dawn's Highway Bleeding ...'

As a child growing up in St. Louis
My father would often quip
"I'm the roughest, toughest, meanest, hombre
this side of the Pecos River, Pard"

I was five years old when we packed up the '48 Dodge
Headed out West via Rte. 66 in 1954
We crossed the Pecos into New Mexico one morning
And following a short stack of hot cakes in Santa Rosa
I asked my father

"Papa, are you the roughest, toughest, meanest, hombre
this side of the Pecos River, too?"

That's when I realized I knew just how to keep the old farts howling

M. I. C., See You Real Soon...

On the lawn above the wall, a fieldstone
facade on 4th Avenue laden
with the similar to wee apricot balls
of fallen fruit which, littered the front yard
of our Bates Motel-like mansion of a rental
where my Boy Scout brother and I posed
and sweltered — The two of us, new to SoCal
towheads, scabby knees and elbows
alongside Rudy Nordquist, the landlord's
marginally gentrified German monster brat

Some poor soul had parked his British
convertible out front. The top, fully retracted
– leather interior exposed and the perfect strike zone
for the Whitey Ford pelting of loquat hurlers
albeit, we were, every one of us
rag-armed righties, we'd nonetheless
make a hell of an unsightly mess
of this little red Austin Healey

A detective I'd later envision as Martin Balsam
rooftop falling, slomo-Hitchcock
You know, *Psycho*-like through the skylight
above our bedroom ... staircase
Investigating a crime of passion
a murder having occurred prior to our moving-in
— purely memoir minutiae, but no shit

And where I'd mouse-like descend, a cartoon of a tiptoe
and a titter to a box of chocolates, an addictive mix
of nuts and cherries, from whence
our father grilled us – me and Gerry
as to who had robbed him of his tasty treasures
an assortment of See's

presented to him on a Christmas eve charter
he'd chauffeured to Fort Apache

I was oh so young - hadn't quite yet perfected
the art of prevarication
If I'd only held out a little longer
my brother may have confessed, displayed
a modicum of honor – I couldn't believe I'd eaten
the entire, assessed accusation

Dad was actually very calm re the issue
gave me a tissue or two to dab up the fear
and the guilt, and although, customarily applied to cursing
my punishment was a sliver of soap to eat
coupled with confinement to our upstairs room
– both, benevolent deserts vis a vis
the infamous work belt ass-whippings
the old man would regularly mete out as we grew older

That evening, dad brought home Lucky Boy burgers
Gerry had asked for two. Dad okayed the order
but, with the caveat that he finish every last morsel
They were huge. Hell, dad could only eat one himself
and Gerry was no Haystacks Calhoun

On the least of the creaky risers, I sat silent
secluded in the stairwell, when my muffled laughter
led to tears, watching my brother gag and regurgitate
I repositioned the mail order mouse ears on top of my head
as that second, half-eaten, hamburger returned to his plate

We lived two blocks from Balboa Park
the year that Annette Funicello stole my brother's heart
and *The Mickey Mouse Club* premiered

The Grigsby Kid

The Grigsby kid was a hard luck kid
Mom and I stood at the kitchen window
Listened to the screech & thud
of anatomy collide with an automobile
— a sound outside that would ever echo
a frightening keepsake from my childhood

Standing just beside her and tugging
at the post-modern print of an apron tied
to the waist of her cotton day dress in gingham
– broccoli, pea pods, and red potatoes
Corn stalking the minefields of juvenile tragedy

I held a fistful of mother's vintage, kitchen attire
trying to get her attention, but lost in a far off vision
All she could image beyond the old purple Caddie
was the broken body of *her* year seven child
The blood from *my* ears pooling in the street

One year later, this same little boy
The Grigsby kid, not *me*, having mended
would slam a Gothic-windowed door
– the pane of which would shatter, and the shards
would slash his arm like pie dough rolled
into a swirl of raspberry batter

De Anza Cove

Pachucos played mumbly-peg
on the barrio stoops, brandished
bone-handled switchblades – stilettos
bootlegged across *la frontera*
but most commonly on display
"sharp and shiny"
in the downtown pawn shop windows
— those lining the leatherneck
and squid liberty streets of our portside city
Back then, all of this, in relative proximity
to my summer days spent
at Our Lady of the Rosary

An eight yard, GMC flatbed truck
with slatted, Western Cedar sides
transported us – children who'd
rode upon ass cracks rife
with the prickly, tickling torture
of wet sand, and in suits still damp
sat and squirmed, chassis-bounced
aloft the worn bearing grind
of this vehicle's noisy rear axle

Unsecured on the floorboards of its
creaking, splintery ride
We didn't have to abide so sensibly
so cautiously, for the dearth of existing
safety laws back then
—those limited to nonexistent
having little or no liability while
moms and dads thought better of having
their brats bored and underfoot all summer
wearing down the nap of the carpets
in the rentals they could barely afford

They shipped me off for the greater part of each day
(and I might add, for the sake of their sanity)
to a churchy li'l summer camp down by the bay
— a Catholic enclave a block or two
south of Little Italy. The sisters there all wore habits

And though it may have been a financial strain
on my parents, due, as I look back
to the modicum of means they'd possessed
The other kids who'd attended were likewise
not of the dregs, but of a similar social caste
That is to say, we'd all eaten breakfast to begin our days
even if it was only a couple of buttered tortillas

"Sarasponda" was one of the songs
I remember singing in that truck and go figure
"Jimmy Crack Corn" and "The Crawdad Song"
(You Get a Line and I'll Get a Pole)
We had chaperones, counselors who'd taught us
to swim that summer – all at the cost of torsos
a medium rare in the blistering sun
Out to a buoy and back. It was the first time
we'd seen a turd afloat upon the water

It alarmed us so…out of its context of a toilet bowl
Disgustingly animated and among us
buoyant and bobbing — some of the children
it touched …were sobbing, hysterical, frenzied —
a siren even sounded. Evacuation, an immediate
imperative. We watched two lifeguards
who'd been alerted, and who'd held the responsibility
of fishing-out the infrequent release of feces
while concurrently, tending to a child
on the shoreline stung, by a small, mottled Round Ray
feeding in the shallows

That's when our soggy, gritty, tuna salad sandwiches
would unravel – where our dry, briny dusted lips
and grainy teeth readied beneath the stark, dappled
lapping irradiance that would sigh and leech
at the whispering tides of De Anza Cove
near Belmont Park at Mission Beach

That same summer, in the company of some other boys
spying on our bellies and taking turns peeping through
the engineering generosity of vents at the base
and before the female communal changing rooms

– where I was to discover, young and old, hairless and hairy
These girls did *not* have penises. Actually, it appeared
they were missing something, or so it struck me
a very analytical seven year old

The Hotel Cecil

What we were doing in downtown Los Angeles in 1962
is far from the shallows of my recollection

The 1920's flair of stone facades and majestic marble columns
were in eerie contrast to the peculiar placement
of its wrought iron fire escape frontage

The Greyhound Station wasn't far away. They'd
put my Dad up there for the night
on many occasions. He'd driven to and fro
for so many years out of San Diego ...
drove one of those swift scenic-cruising, machinations

From the inner city outer limits, across the nation, Yes
the depot wasn't very far from the Stay on Main
or better known to the downtown locals
as "The Suicide Cecil"

Nearby Eighth Street was skid row, for which
my father always had a strange fascination
One that he passed on to my brother and me, ergo
our would-be obsessions with the Beats – Ginsberg
Ferlinghetti, & Bill, the celebrated urban junky, Burroughs

The hotel of 600 rooms or so had been the focus
of copious, terrible atrocities: serial murders, rapes
dismemberments, etcetera; but most infamously
it owned the reputation of suicide central

To wit, a young woman had just leapt from a window
on or above the room that dad had booked
for Gerry and me ... up on the ninth floor
and to make matters worse, she'd lit on another

Landed directly on a passerby, resulting
in a collateral mishap, sort of an immediate, mortal encore

Most of the dwellers there were transients, eroded
no doubt by addiction. They were hopelessly lacking
in a future of any quality to speak of. I can see now
how suicide might have been an appropriate option
for these – the walking non-fictional dead

As frightening as the whole experience was to us as children
holed-up in that seedy little room (for the night)
Our crazy old man of a sire
still felt the urge to further intensify our angst
when he decided to perform his version
of a groveling drunk— twisting the knob of our chained
albeit, unbolted door

Dad, in the hotel hallway, slurring the words, "Let me in!"
The chilling din of his bedraggled gait – scraping the foyer floor

Feigning Innocence

A maple stump that fails to mask
The musk of my labor
Even enhances
The odor of my toil
Which I do not find offensive

And further, this odor I own
Sends me on a journey back to 1958
To the sizzle of burgers on the grill
In an antique of a train car diner
Juxtaposed to Mercy
And the genesis of Old CA-395

My parents would take us there
After a double feature of westerns and war
On the road home
I'd play with my mother's ponytail
Falling asleep with it
Draped on my face

I'd wake to the dreamy scent
Of night-blooming jasmine and sage
My father would cradle me
Like a gorilla across the lawn
The scuffs of his worn-black, work boots
Sopped with crabgrass dew

Beneath the nip
In that clear night sky
I'd feign the innocence of being ten
I'd whisper to him
Crafted echoes
On clouds of visible breath

Brownie

Bob Brown was a Greyhound Bus driver
and a friend to our father. One evening
Bob encouraged dad to drink
Jim Beam with him after work. He brought
dad home in a cab and took him into the
bathroom. Mom told us, Gerry and me
to go to our room – that dad was sick
We heard him howling in the cold shower

Bob would bring his wife, Cora
over to our house for dinner and drinks
They had two half-Comanche daughters
one of whom, I loved and played
kiss in the closet with

Bob played football in the street with me
and my neighborhood friends. He could
run like Jim Thorpe. Bob Brown was the best
golfer dad knew in San Diego. He won all
of the Greyhound tournaments and
hustled the municipal courses on his days off

Bob was wild, loved to swill whiskey
and womanize. Dad was leery of these traits

Bob Brown died early in his life from a heart
attack . . . too many shots on the basketball
court. We lost both of them to heart disease
actually . . . for Bob, it was mixing spirits
with sports. For dad, it was his gluttony
for depot and truck stop grease

The Wailing of Cats

Back from the farm with a crate of eggs
They fit my hand so well
So perfectly in my palm
I'd hurl one of the unborn
fifty-five yards
Right after Mama
laid upon us the whiskered kisses
from her old prickly lips
Onto us, the *Brothers Katzenjammers*
Ever the Halloween hobos, Hans *und* Fritz
Und ve ver aus ... gone slinging
the gravel rackets of corrugated patio thunder
Its din a derivative of the thrill
for raising hell

Like cats in heat
We'd beat the stench
from the metal trash cans in the street
Rolling them down the avenues
where colonial white doors dripped
the viscous licorice wads of a charcoal chew
better known to us back then
as Thomas Adam's blackjack spit
... running down, down

...down from the tall
dormant October grasses
& into the light of the dark
cold foggy moon
where little league leathernecks
lobbed raw egg grenades
Pummeled pillbox mansions
und der Inspector's *haus*

... ran down to the elementary school
to the PTA arcades

Our chests, homing the heaving carnival hearts
starved of innocence, yet replete with impish delight
The more malice we managed – the louder our laughter

... after which, a fight broke out in front of the girls
One of the clever toms, "the poet" had facetiously pondered
Then stated without stammer -
> *When swollen breasts were firmly squeezed*
> *From nipples there should trumpet cheese*

Thereafter, ensued a peal of *katzenjammer*

We were at war with the adults that night
Nothing they could say
would calm our bedeviled spirits
Young constructs of the Fallen Angel
und der Inspector
The latter, would set a curfew
that we'd both marvel and scoff at

... and thus
We stayed out far past midnight
and finished off the school
Evened the score
with some of the neighbors
and the resident teachers who'd
put targets on our backs
Spurned us for defying irrelevant rules
... stayed out
with the rest of the damned
to further punish
the already slumbering parents of kids

who'd done something once
that would mark them for unending mischief

We crouched and sprang, hissed in the caves
against the foreboding darkness of hillsides
Baring our claws like a gang of zealots, mittens
burning at a bonfire rally

... *Rally all ye nasty rascals*
Ye pack of animals on the prowl
Growling at the babies with their goody bags
Mouths agape with savage columns
of candy corn teeth — exhibits of sticky niblets
Mewling on the twisted arms of an old oak tree

The black and the orange of calicos cackling
Candles flickering in a window of eyes
Where the jack o'-lanterns
nefarious railings of silent fright
were further muted by the howling bluster
of another nippy, nor'easter night

On the following autumnal morn
if attendance was required
We'd be hung-over from the exuberance
likely truant for the delinquency
and the pride we'd find difficult to hide
... stifling the previous, hallowed eve's
demolitions, damnations with lies

We'd be forced to wear blinders
– covers for our ornery eyes
Orbs that may have been unable
to still the unhinging of genuine glee
For all of the school's windows

wore streaks of Palmolive, and the Kiwi
shoe polish pictorials
that waxed lascivious and went hand in glove
with scripts endemic to the malicious
polemics of our lewd manifesto

And though, in the aftermath
we did attend – were subject to witness
the disgust in the demeanor
of an off-duty custodian
His misery for the tedium
tickled us pink – coming in on his day off
wethinks … or thought that is
to remove the smear and the smudge, to toil
with the sediment of our sedition
graffiti that spoke to a grudge
we held against the structure, an edifice
named for a stuffy old bastard
with a monocle against his eye
& a hearing aid to the ear of our defiance

We had a vendetta for the faculty's vigilance
to nuance and, of course, the formidable inquisitions
von der Inspector – who'd been brought in
so many times before and fed so very well
He was proficient in his methods
for gleaning confidence and information
Exacting from a preponderance of the doughtiest
Particularly in the neighboring prides
but we'd been sworn to fealty
and thus, were his thwarted efforts
to make *our* big cats cry

Number One Seed

My dad had promised me a trip to the Y one day when I was about thirteen because I'd complained to him that my table tennis game was suffering in the confines of our garage. We were already playing about even-steven, though he had the edge as I recall, with his snappy backhand

Having collided with lawn mowers and tool chests, golf clubs, etc., I insisted I could return his slams with greater frequency provided I had a few more feet around the table. Dad was always willing to accommodate me and my desire to better him on a level playing field, so

We embarked on a day trip to San Diego some seventeen miles from where we'd resided in El Cajon. As it turned out, I did excel with the extra area around the table but his proficiency seemed to heighten as well, due in part as I look back, to the competitive nature of our relationship. That is to say, I played harder and he responded with a likewise, elevated effort

Now there was this sailor (dad would call him a *swabby*) who was sidling around the table, almost getting in the way of our play. I could see dad getting a wee bit irritated by this young buck in his white get-up. It was pretty apparent he wanted to be a participant in our little father-son Sunday afternoon competition, and finally, rather aggressively, requested to play the winner of the next match

We'd played at least six matches at this point and dad, always game and fit, showed the signs of wear on account of his inability to put me away so quickly with his offense. So, as the story goes, the *swabby* got his way … and I mean *really* got his way. I pitied my dad for the beating he took and loathed this acned seapunk for his incredible forehand which had pinpoint accuracy

He was virtually devoid of a backhand so, to compensate, he positioned himself to the extreme left of center. Dad worked at handcuffing him and was, on occasion, successful, but the young seaman spun the ball in a way that kept Dad's returns to the right the majority of the time

Dad looked at me with desperation in his eyes. He was soaked with perspiration. I began to choke-up, you know, my emotions were welling-up in my throat, and I could see this asshat grinning and enjoying his advantage with a despicable, post-adolescent arrogance. In my mind I saw myself wielding my 30 oz. Louisville Slugger, connecting with the sweet spot on his forehead. I felt his teeth shatter ... nose cave... eyes explode... ego deflate, but all I could *really* do was glower like I'd done when the *Pachuco* kicked my brother in the knee down at the playground

Dad lost three games and we headed home. He said the sailor was a shitbird, but even in his younger days wouldn't have been a match for this guy. I always thought dad was the best I'd ever seen – and I still do

Tumescent Pleasures

Painting their toes
 on a concrete stoop
High school girls
 chided my approach
"Freddy, Freddy
 Let's go steady"
 they smirked
Fags dangled
from the pink stucco
 of their lower lips
Bucked on each hard syllable

They were ruthless
 with my pubescent psyche
Cheap and sexy
 their legs and underarms
exposed a pepper stubble
 Images
that I would reference
 when routine
would arouse me
To that which
 I'd recently become
educated in
And thus, addicted to
 One boy's
life-altering revelation
of autoerotic recreation

So
with my grubby little
stripling mitts
I'd masturbate
 in a cave of boulders
across the street

Or on the floor
 of a plywood shack
that we'd nailed
to some eucalyptus trees
I'd sit there
 and stroke the magic lamp
Jeans
 just above my knees
Beside a sticky stack
of damp
Corrugated
Playboy Magazines

Janie

Capturing the attention of
every pimpled, gangly
neighborhood knucklehead
and some of the fathers too
Janie would pedal up and down
the avenues of our named
for the avian, residential tract
She lived in a cookie-cutter house
on Dove Street
at the curve in the *cul-de-sac*

One day she appeared
in our driveway, a tomboy
in her shears-frayed denim shorts
An open-ended wrench, fixed
in the snug posterior
of her skin-tight, rear patch pocket
and beneath the shroud of her old man's
muscular sleeveless, tired-at-the-neckline
terrycloth sweatshirt

Sagging much the same as the chain that draped
from the sprocket of her two-toned Schwinn
when she rolled the cream
and lavender up the ramp
An unbefitting grin featured
upon her face – confused me
as I finished with a rabid forehand
placed against my competition of drywall

Surprised in this absence of a pall, I offered
an awkward, if plausible, "Hello Smiley"
We'd engaged with sweaty hands
at the middle school dance
and, in earlier days, cuddled in the nuanced
nooks and crannies of hide and seek

At fourteen she'd been regaled
with a divine profile, a lovely set
of breasts, generally, most generously
on display for the imagination

but on this day, she'd leaned over
to gift me with an unveiling
and while memory still serves me
I can see them
slightly swaying in revelation

A momentous still of her treasured chest
— frame of flesh that teased my teenage brain
Drove me a tad insane when suddenly
she stopped fiddling with her filthy chain
and stood, as my mother appeared, arms akimbo
— a silhouette in the screen door

Mom asked me later at the dinner table if I'd had a good look

Black Sheep

Mom bolted out of the house and into the street
to keep an older boy from beating me up for a baseball
She like to have broken my arm with all of the wringing power
in her wrists. This kid was two years older, bigger
and had the edematous, clammy hands
he liked to push in your face; fingernails chewed to the quick
He was not a friendly sort — uncomfortable in his own skin, they'd say
The prototype of a mesomorph with a mien enhanced by a strict
regimen of lifting heavy weights and running sprints
and while he already had a learners' permit, bowled a perfect game
subbing for his dad in a men's league; he was an awkward bully
devoid of the facility for shame. And even though
he was an outstanding athlete, most of the neighborhood kids
preferred he play on the opposing team

I wasn't shy in the street but knew this kid well for his dearth of humility
So, when he claimed ownership of my baseball, and all the kids
were watching, I squared-off with him, anticipating contact
with those thick wet mitts. The real abashment resulted when
my mother stormed out to rescue me from a beating by this guy
It was just wrong. My father's advice was even worse. "Take a bat to this kid"
"That's the way you balance the scales." I'd realize later that the old man
would never have done that, and I'd seen a kid smacked with a bat
— a practice swing near the backstop during recess. It was an accident
that made me sick, and besides, this very large kid was a black sheep
He'd suffered enough already

Free Drinks

Two or three miles over the rolling, bouldered
barrel-cacti, jackrabbit hills, just southwest of Santee
where my best friend and I back in those days, practiced our talents
for being scamps — rotten little rascals with a love
of carbonation, and the ideal template for sampling
the exaggerated sweetness of spritzing libations, discovered
in an old-fashioned soda pop machine
situated supine on a dirty, dead end backroad, located
near the grandstands at the horse ranch stables
of Fletcher Hills

We carried with us the tools of the craft – a bottle top popper
and a straw, the latter modified with an extended shaft
conferring upon us …that certain ease of access, and thus
we'd fill our eager gobs. One of us would prop open the cooler door
after having popped the top from a flavored drink, while the other
would lay prostrate across the chest, slightly sink
and suck until his cheeks turned sore; chilling with a Fanta, a Nehi
or a Hires, methinks …any in a myriad of options desired

So, with this uber tube of a straw to our mouths, we'd siphon
and flood our bellies with fizzy fluids – leaving nary a doubt we'd
sucked-up all the free soda we could

As luck would have it, I'd already had my turn at the wrest, when my mate
came up with an extemporaneous confession, one so incredulously lame…
and yet, curiously rare, having been nabbed — caught red-handed
by the head of the horsemen there. He couldn't just face the music and take
the rap, not without this further distension, "I'm sorry sir, but I've never had
one of those before." I burst into laughter. "Get the hell out of here"
the horseman spat. We shuffled off … then broke into a full sprint

Killing Time

The granite boulders are currently
the townhouses & the condominiums
Tainted, counterfeit paintings
from a gallery of serial murders
— slayers of chronology and sketches
descending into delineations of non-fiction
where factual depictions of neighborhoods
have been erased of the rife with vicious rascals
incendiaries responsible for a very glaring
catalog of memories – like the time a torch
was put to a tumbleweed on the fly, ablaze
in the fan of a Santa Ana Indian summer bluster
... and then
there was a guy who'd nearly lost his eye
doubling for Vic Morrow — reenacting
a *Combat* episode with his pellet rifle
and a sack of granite grenades
We, who'd pelt and were pelted with solids
of sediment, dirt clods and the horseshit grubbed
from the crust of the SoCal soil
Hurlers, who'd hurled everything
we could get our hands on out there
where I'd hid a pack of my father's fags
that some other freckled little shit found
in a boulder crevice, and who'd
smoked and smoldered with them
one by one in the grains of the yellow wavy
And o'er those fields of meadowlarks
and doves fluttering from the shrubby dust of sage
... of the tribal wars we'd wage
with our premeditated devices
initially bought for the bubble-eyed amusement
but were later implements for the insecticidal
schemata of total annihilation — a magnifying
glass brought out and brandished

as a bellicose declaration against the calderas
of the red ants vis a vis the black ants
Megalopolistic formicaries besieged
by the giant children of the earth

Out there – in the wonderfully, otherworldly
natural cacti and coyote playground that God
and the paychecks of a Greyhound Bus driver
had provided us
Across Cuyamaca Street, where metal shops
and the plethora of industrial edifices now stand
once stood the stands of eucalypti
& groves of pepper and oak
– its host of wildlife bulldozed-over
by the murderous machinery of time

Pigeonholed

The El Cajon Police chased Danny and me from
a railroad car full of Monkey Ward's merchandise
foiled our attempts to break the lock with a pry bar
in order that we might reenact the lives of the hobos
we'd dreamed up – stolen excerpts from a book
my brother was reading

The police took us down to the station in a black
and white – my handcuffed, bone-bruised wrists
had my father so pissed when he came in for me
I thought he would barrel-chest one of those bastards
grapple with him onto the floor and break a cheekbone
or a nose with his hard-ass, bus-driving right fist —
but we were living in the real world and he was only
capable of later rubbing my wrists with salve. He
called me Capone for a couple of weeks and restricted
me for the alleged, attempted robbery – and something
else I'd done at school that had gotten me
suspended temporarily

From that time on, until I was eighteen, anything
and everything reported missing in that neighborhood
Danny and I'd be suspect for – called in for questioning
grilled and put in the hot seat, until my dad petitioned
an ostensibly reasonable administrator at the central
station, and who'd subsequently have the incident
expunged from my record some years later, so I could
enlist in the United States Marine Corps, go off to that
farcical war in Southeast Asia ... shit
I'd have been better off, an ineligible thief

Grey Cedar Farmhouse Weekend Sleepover

These people — the Rooneys
were dear to me
Rex, the patriarch
was a Greyhound dispatcher
and the sire to an Irish clan
of Howdy Doody redheads
One of whom, I'd shared a bed with
— my friend, Mike
the freckled son and nail biter
Impersonator of the Verne Gagne
vise grip trademark sleeper hold
His jockey shorts were streaked
with the sienna buck sergeant stripes
of an eleven year old in a big hurry
His bed was dirtier than mine
had an odor of other than me
His linens were stiff
with far too much starch … and gritty

Downstairs, the Rooneys
like livestock slumbered – They woke
and broke me from my dreams and silence
with a Morse Code of apnea snorts

The day before, we'd played on boulders
off of Pepper Drive and Tuttle Lane
miles from our separate schools
but mere minutes from our dentist
whose atrocious halitosis
seemed a far greater infliction
than his practice of no-Novocain
drilling into raw nerve

We'd spied on him in his basement
applying small, taut rubber bands
to baked ceramic molds, one of them
a model of my large rodent overbite
and replica of my stupid grin
— all jackal-jawed on a workshop shelf
seated next to the myriad
and equally, stupid adolescent grins
in his menagerie
of hysterical malocclusions

And on that day
we ran like tumbleweeds
pushed by the wind
chased by a small pack
of snarling hounds into a grove
of rotten shimmy poles
following our taunts to a wallowing drift
of squealing Pietrain Hogs
in their pens

And when we
further upon a warren fell
– that element of surprise
had the jump-out of jackrabbits
put a spark to our spines

With a few of Mike's lazy
summertime pals, who'd merely tagged along
we hid in the hillside rattlesnake sage
One set of binoculars for the four of us
aimed on the volleyball nudists
at a weekend nature retreat
… in a canyon, past cottonwood
and molting eucalyptus

The security, an unclad enforcer
secured his lopsided testicles
with a shroud of camouflage loincloth
…chased us with a B.B. rifle
and a battle cry
while the crippled kid among us
oblivious to his handicap
of schlepping a defective limb
– kept himself abreast of our flight
fueled by super jolts of adrenaline

From the dust and the broken sage
– our *terra firma* exodus … of this
a boyhood planet playground
of granite undulations
Its slightly acrid sap of trees
coalesced with the scent
of freshly painted stables
where an old nag would hose us down
with a wrought-up blast of equine sneeze

Our evening meal of meatloaf
… took respite in a tulip field
dressed in the classic ketchup glaze
resting there where windmill vanes
churned peas and mashed potatoes
on the glossy, blue and ivory
– semblance of delftware plates

Under the rosewood dining table
our filthy-naked, played-out feet
luxuriated in the spinal shag
of the Rooney's spent mutt, Rusty
– a geriatric at thirteen

I remember hiding my peas
in the mashed potatoes
– the method, by which I eat them today
Mike's younger sister, Cathy
always thought that I was so damned

clever and cute for the slightest
innovations I'd introduce
and at eleven years old
it made me uneasy – but queasier yet
was I when I stepped barefoot
upon one of Rusty's furtive land mines

– the serpentine coil of the old dog's dump
gave like a well-cooked candied yam
– hidden beneath a veil of Bermuda grass clippings
I could not wash that foot enough
…and the release of the god-awful smell…
Mike began bleeding from the exaggerated
lip-stretching laughter he'd been avoiding
for most of the day
A chronic condition he'd acquired
required balm be applied whenever we'd play

Mike and I would continue to comb
the hills of Santee and El Cajon
for a few more years
chucking rocks at ground squirrels
and meadowlarks, jackrabbits
and the presumably abandoned
warehouse windows near Gillespie Field

Hell, we shook the hand of LBJ in 1960
at a rally the Dems had held out there

It was all banners and brass
and the Lady Bird; Lyndon even wore
a ten gallon hat, which was slightly absurd
on account of the decorum seemed contrary
to running on the ticket with JFK

It was all the free weenies
we could fit in our gobs
Mike naturally wolfed-down five
of those dawgs far too quickly
Puked into a box full of campaign brochures
declaring *A new leader for the 60's*

I pedaled home on my Huffy
– pumped my cruiser up the *verboten*
Cuyamaca Street, where I glimpsed
my dad in the picture window
waiting to tan my ass with his work belt

Rex was granted a transfer
and moved his family to Phoenix
They put old Rusty down
when his legs gave out
That was the end of our hijinks
Mike Rooney and me
I heard that his dad got him a job
as a baggage handler
in the inferno of Tempe or was it Mesa
– slaving in the oppressive heat
before he'd turn 21
but a lot of us bad boys
would enter the Gates of Hell in '68

Long Before I Knew the Rifleman Was a Dodger

He was one of those dumpy old bastards
obviously trying to knock it out of a child's ballpark
200 feet to the scoreboard in center
from where he stood at the plate
He'd swing three times through every ball
before he'd make contact and we laughed
Guffawed at the cap spinning off of his barren crown
Thank you Bozo - Next year bring the red nose

Subsequently, we'd lost our focus
or at least I did when
I was hit in the ear with a one bounce shot
a rope off of this dummy's bat
My ear lobe wore the ephemeral impression
of Spalding seams. I was glad though I hadn't been
smacked with one of those hard, cheap
funny rubber bouncing balls
the league had often purchased in bulk
for the annual baseball tryouts

The veteran coaches of World War II and Korea
thought it was a good lesson for any youth –
maybe one day it would be a grenade
That was the inane postbellum wisdom
in El Cajon Valley, and probably
all over the country in the late 1950s
I was well-deserving of that puffy
red ringing cartilage – that helix-stung-like-hell of an ear

Heads-up goddamn it! The car salesman sneered
Get your head in the game, kid! The sawyer barked
That'll wake your ass up, knucklehead! The mechanic choked
— hocked-up a lunger that bounced in the dirt

One of them would call me later that afternoon
interrupting the kitschy dialogue between
Chuck Connors and Johnny Crawford
… tell me I'd made the Mustangs, the where
and the what time of our first practice

I would be ecstatic as I switched the receiver to my un-iced ear

Happy Birthday Sir, September 12, 1957

I reach for the coffee cup with my father's hand
A relief of liver spots, cast against the hills and valleys
of knuckles and joints; a confluence of blue streams
coursing the follicular sun bleach of a manual forest
each digital movement, a serpent wriggling in the rise
of the weathered crepes of vein
Listening to myself, giving one of his – unabashed
dining room table refrains – *mea pater verbatim*

As if it was yesterday, I could sense him readying for work
The creaking hide at his side held a ticket punch and a changer
– the latter, a trickling din of coinage released with the spillage
of silver and copper a 'clatter. Clutching his leather brief –
home to a continuous flow, at least an inch thick sheaf of union
grievances, sworn against the administration. He'd kiss the mouths
of my mother and me — emanations of Listerine
and the Chesterfields he'd smoke; a hint of aftershave, Old Spice or
was it Jade East that smelled so nice, even appealing, although ...

On one of our celebrated evenings, he'd give my brother and me
a beating. Sort of went berserk on us with his broad, coal-black
cowhide, work belt. Strapping us beneath the blue strain
of a face contorted, distorted with something more than mere discipline
Maybe a form of divine madness had inspired the ailing, fatherless
soul of our sire – possibly aflame with one of those ... Grecian fires
of *theia mania*

I remember my brother and I'd been fighting during a visit from our
friend and neighbor, Mr. Huff, I believe. He'd come over to share
a birthday libation, when father found brother disrobing
ready to enter the tub, and me — I was on the rowdy rodeo spread

neatly splayed across my bed … when the old man snapped
and we were savagely strapped, beaten from our buttocks
to the backs of our thighs; such was the immediate rise revealing
a painful asymmetry – its ruby-red wealth of rosehips, already aglow
before those beatings were over, and in the aftermath, a blue and black
sundry would show into the depths of October

El Cajon Valley

The '46 Hudson took sanctuary
from the heat in the shade
of a shedding pepper tree, pink pods
stirred on a warm breeze in the gutter

Playing catch with the old man
at Passover was … subjecting
myself to the subsequent
rancid hamburger

redolence derived
from the god-awful
farewell armpit embraces
of my father's father

His cold grey
glove compartment revolver
sat holstered in red leather
atop a map of El Cajon Valley

A Mitzvah

Hot for my auntie who was 16
when she allowed me passage aboard –
granted me permission to dry hump the camel
when we'd feign the untoward wrestling
Rather taboo was the view before the eyes
of my motherly matron, who'd long ago
rendered the lock to my bedroom door defunct

Auntie would nonetheless
slip out of her jailhouse blouse
and swab me down with her glistening
just-back-from-juvie jugs
Her stained-with-breast-sweat bra
crushed and rubbed
my cherubic cheekbones raw
Under her udderly dank and musty
mammalian globes afire
The inner coals of her body burning
She rather stank with the human teenage
carnal desires, sadistically discerning

and with the strong hot digits
of her *Strawberry Delighted*, fingernails peeling
Held me in a bondage of reddened wrists
Pinned me down and indian-rubbed me
Outweighed me 30 pounds
The copper zipper pinched my frenulum

Just 12 years old and beginning to understand
the wonders of this psychosexual tension
That damned lusty, seductive scent
from the powerful, the steamy; the axial stubble
of my prurient aunt. I tasted a bead

of her Semitic sweat – essence of jezebel
from the salt mine

Goddess mistress woman girl who'd reek for me a pleasure
that had me reveling from the ailing side of my brain

No one would call it perverting the lobe but me
It was all mine, every Passover – 'twas a *mitzvah!*

The Dressing Room

He ruled the roost. Even when it came to my threads
my school clothes, that is, if you're slightly slow
on the slang, meathead. He'd call me that, too
We shopped at Fedmart in the buzzy mid-afternoon
shitfly heat of El Cajon Valley ... sort of like Costco
or Sam's Club; me, mom and The King

My brother was already off performing the Beatnik
in San Francisco, pounding on his own chest
of bongos with his new wife, Babs of obscene
nude acrylic fame — family scandal of Beulah Street
near Kezar Stadium. Her tangled canvas mass
of a jungly auburn bush, contoured the minds
of the repressed, impromptu relatives of pop-in
unannounced, visitor legacy — drooling avuncular
albeit, wholesome churchy boner hypocrites
all a 'twitter
... and the old man, well, he was the expert
on all things fitting and proper, especially when it came to
styling a youngster of thirteen — aptly providing the attire
concurrent with a middle school theme. O Lordy, he was
so like hep back then. Really hep to all of the clothing
and tonsorial trends — crew cuts always in vogue and the pure
manifest of a clean mind covered with a baseball cap, a mind
that lived by the Little League Pledge:
I trust in God – I love my country and will respect
its laws – I will play fair and strive to win but win
or lose, I will always do my best. Ah, the glory of it all!
Five years later, I'd be pledging in opposition to the bayonet drills
at MCRD, "Kill VC," I'd scream ... but I digress

I despised him so for the tyranny and the omniscience. That's why
I jumped at every opportunity to make a monkey out of him, and thus
I wrote a little ditty, a dressing room song which goes something like this

I tried on a pair of trousers
One that all of the so-called, "cool heads" wore
...it draped so perfectly
on my identity crisis, and not to mention
my psyche sore
and alas upon my callow physique
my preadolescent awkward scape oblique

Didactic and whereupon with diction wise
the king denied me, and then decried:
"These are the pants I'll have you wear
and this is the size ... I do not share
the length you think ... is "out of sight"

So son, get back in there and put these on
– Go on! ... into the dressing room. Don't piss away my day!
Go on back in there and take these!
They'll fit far better, given the length of your scrawny legs
... your boney knees!

So I took his selection of trousers, two sizes too small
into that dressing room
Hung them overhead on a brass hook
while the ones I'd preferred
remained tenaciously zipped
and buttoned to my slender frame

I think I picked my nose and flicked
a dried booger onto the floor
Sat there lamenting for a minute or two
Rose and opened the curtain door

Voila! I did a couple of pirouettes for the old prick
As he assured me then, that I was certainly attending
to a far better fit; a comelier look
"Now, that's much better" followed a puff of smoke
from his Chesterfield cigarette

Riverwalk

Traversing the length of that trestle, ironed recumbent
on the Anaheim sky, where my cousin and I
gleaned with trepid awareness, a perilous view
a muddy flow where the sunshine glare
dappled below the span of those railroad tracks
illusively narrowing with distance

And harrowing was the fear of coasters coming at
or onto us from our rear
Cow plowing us
before we could climb down and explore the stanchions
for the nomadic inscriptions – the Kilroy graffiti on the pockmarked
girth of concrete footings

And prior to the brown gangs tagging & taking over
the underworld of the freeways, chasing the journeymen
from their jungles and staking claim to the outlaw freedoms
of those, tattered itinerant scribes

Under the overpass, the charred remains; a few of those
orange crates with Oxnard labels, & alongside
the typical trash of tramps – their detritus
of sardine tins and stubbed-out stogies, blackened remnants
of campsite coals and ash

I guess those gnarly old free birds vanished, found work
in the fields and factories somewhere, nearby or faraway

Forty years would pass before my cousin would gift me
with a railroad treasure, a spike he'd kept in *homage*
to those fond memories we had together — playing chicken
with an iron horse, high above the Santa Ana River

Cajon Speedway

The relationship of grandstands rife with the rabid yen
elevated appetites for far less than a dearth of chewy, crunchy
snacks – inverse to the flashing and the banshee wailing
of emergency vehicle sirens tending
to the possible death or disembodiment of speedway mishaps

The intake of food to the outpouring of blood
was a lesson in humanity for me … at what, sixteen, it would
assuage my misanthropic desires for seclusion, coupled
with the crippling psychoses neuroses of returning
from the slaughter of war, just four years later

Bottles of pop in buckets of ice. I'd become muscular and callused
— my strong, svelte limbs in absolute opposition to the weak
projection of my voice, a handicap that would keep me from earning
the money and the respect for myself I'd needed that summer

I worked for Leo, the concessioner. Don and Crusty, my peers
were likewise vendors, the former secured a position for me there
One day he'd become a world-renowned asteroseismologist
— discoverer of pulsating stars

... That I Would Cheat That Poor Old Woman

Over the many years
we lived in San Diego County
granny would stay with us
from time to time, slept in the converted
sewing room

when she wasn't working as a Harvey Girl
at the Grand Canyon, or waiting tables
at Clifton's in downtown Los Angeles
She was feisty but fragile
had osteoporosis and social security

We became fierce competitors
on account of the idleness we shared, me
a bored teen, searching for an identity
and she, menopausal and without a man in her life

Chinese checkers, gin rummy, old maid
The latter, prompted my jests, japes
'of the game being created at her behest'
We should've been playing old divorcee
A more befitting game, copyright pending
as four times forlorn in wedlock was she

Future lung cancers were of no concern
when grandma sent a carton of Winston's to me
sleeping with rats in the charred mountainside bunkers
of *Quang Tri*, a little more than a stone's throw
from the DMZ in 1968

"Here, if Charlie don't gitcha', these will"
the Christmas card (should've) read
but lest I deviate, it was the game of cribbage
or as we called it, *crib* ... about which, I'd like to relate

...that I would cheat – gain leverage by carefully
focusing on the lenses of my grandmother's
spectacles – stealing reflections of what she'd
held in her hand

From that lighted vantage point, I knew just how
to play my cards, pegging and tossing, though
admittedly I didn't always employ this method
as it involved a sort of ethics issue, at times
a crisis for me

and depending on the bipolarity of my psyche
on certain days, the side abiding by a prevailing
moral code may have encouraged me to acquiesce
act unto that of my Southern Baptist mode

I was a middle-aged man, living with my wife
and children in Anchorage when I received the news
that granny was near the end of her days
Wasting away with dementia in a nursing home
in Peoria, or Tempe, Arizona

I took my jigsaw and drill to a 2x6
shaped her a cribbage board to resemble
a spawning sockeye (salmon), flew down to see her
with her great grandson - down to say so long
in the dog days of August, 1987

when I presented her with what I'd contoured
...120 perforations spanning the still life – twisted
torso strain of a Red Salmon, a game board
with a green felt backing

One of my tears, a droplet, fell from the end of my nose
I'd failed to hold back the sentiments to save my son
from the sadness, for the cold, 70 lbs. of what remained
While abed and behind a floral curtain, the roomie ate
soft boiled eggs with grandma's removable dentures
choppers that a tattooed, *Latina* caregiver had placed
in her mouth by mistake

Flat on her back with this rather absurd passing gift
resting upon her abdomen. A shrunken, hair-barren head
with the sunken eyes of an ancient, slightly propped
and upward peering, she winked at me and weakly said

"I used to play this game with my grandson, Fred"

Mid-Century Sketch

The neighborhood lawn-cutter
and shoeshine boy
my hands smelled of fresh Bermuda
and feet – the feet of the brats that I'd fought
in the *cul-de-sacs*, on the playgrounds
in the tetherball pits.
Kicking, choking, spitting
You'd seldom see these guys
with tears in their eyes
There weren't too many of those
More times than not
it was mere blood and snot
from freckled noses flowed

With the residue of black wax
— of the Kiwi caked beneath my nails
I'd set upon a course of skin endeavors
Evidenced by the callused placement
of seventy-five pounds
behind a well-oiled push mower

My grip was strong
from squeezing clippers and filing blades
These were the hands that held up pockets
sagging with silver and copper
and sort of swaying with the weight
of a mint's depiction
– buffaloes, chiefs and president generals
Glorified national symbols
of colonial imperialism
Memorials to the butchery
on the blood-stained, native plains

I toted a homemade shoe shine kit
In it: a mangled, jaundiced, copy
of *The Adventures of Huckleberry Finn*
2 Camel straights that I'd robbed from "Old Pap"
and a bottle top popper
for the Royal Crown and Nehi machine
down at the Mobil Station

Ever the enterpriser — entrepreneurial miser
I kept a fairly ample sum in a savings account
an amount I religiously considered untouchable
and though I was not a greedy child
I had the nerve to have the purpose
of hoarding for that day

when I would hit the hobo road
where Woody Guthrie played
— played fervor into the grain of my flesh
His pioneer history
strummed region through my veins
The gravelly drawl of his dustbowl refrains
were a prelude to my vision
as a child actor in *The Grapes of Wrath*

America's migrant son, Joadsian-draped
in the frayed and threadbare tatters
Pedaling up and down the blue collar streets
named for common birds
Peddling chutzpah and ambition
on Finch and Heron, Swallow and Dove

Our neighbors were cement truck drivers
and milkmen. Their wives
held Tupperware parties, darned socks

and took in ironing. Together
they sold Amway on the weekends
Some of their sons, my buddies
chucked newspapers from bicycle saddlebags
at five a.m. We all played little league
Curt had a twelve to six curveball
at age thirteen

We were baptized in the ranch style
stucco suburbia that the B of A owned
had older siblings, most of whom
sported ducktails and beehives
(if it didn't fit in their purses, they'd hide it in their hair)

A student of Hemingway and London
I aspired to the tramp life depicted by the "Legends"
Mark Twain and John Steinbeck
I slept with *A Moveable Feast* beneath my pillow

Imagine the excitement I must have known
when my brother turned-me-on to the Beats in '63
and LSD-25 in '67

Sadie Hawkins Dance

I'd attended Santana High School in 1966
35 years prior to the school-shootings out there
I was invited to the Sadie Hawkins dance
after having been duped by a tricky little bitch
a *chica* who'd decided to stick her tongue into my mouth
while sitting on my lap with her perfect little ass
in the crowded back seat of a '56 Ford

After a pep rally or some other unchaperoned
nighttime function, jumping on a trampoline
everyone thought she was somebody's girl, but me
I thought I was in love after I'd swallowed
a jigger of her spit … and on top of that she told me
she'd buy me a ticket to the dance next week
Romance me if I'd let her be my Sadie

While messing with another boy's head, she
gave me the ticket that night, and though the boy
was a Mediterranean green and wanted to kick my ass
he was so goddamned tiny, he decided to pass
But in any case, she ended up dancing with him exclusively
left me pining in the basketball bleachers

with…what the fuck was his name, another boy who'd
come along with me for no apparent reason, and who I knew
from the two years I'd attended Grossmont High. We'd
teamed-up to play outsiders and act the hep cats; like the time
we caught the downtown transit to play pool with the squids
smoke cigarettes and tried to talk shit with the prostitutes
on Imperial. We dreamed we'd have the nerve, pay to get fellated
in the motel of a pimp's parked car

… still trying to believe that one of us was Sal Paradise
on the road to Denver or somewhere (nice), we scrambled
through the moonlight sage and the whipped hips of wavy
warm night tall grass…stumbled over the dark stony barbed wire acreage
at least 5 miles back to Cuyumaca St. and my house on Swallow
where we listened to *Highway 61 Revisited* in high fidelity

Dead Comedians

I'd cleaned the wax from my earphones
Listened to the late night Mystery Theater
Local talk shows, and Wolfman Jack on XERB
Radio Rosarito, my transistor intermittently
broke while I was breaking all the rules

I had school the next day and dad
crawled on his hands and knees
into my bedroom to seize me
by my legs. The old fucker could really
sneak in there and scare the shit out of me
Then he'd laugh for twenty minutes
over giving me a start

He went back into their bedroom
Told me to turn off the radio and get some sleep
resumed with a chuckle or two, then
full-on laughter … belly-laughter
Mom began laughing, too … "Harry!"
And then grandma took the baton
from her bed in the sewing room
… fetching the funny bone, as it were
Thank the good Lord for laughter

I hadn't yet developed the gauche, adolescent
sensitivity that I'd later be stricken with
when I turned the radio off
put a pillow over my head
to drown-out the maniacal din
that played throughout the 1275 square feet
of suburban ranch style habitation

Finally, a harbinger of a tear ran the span
from my eye to the flattened lobe of my ear
It had begun to run into the abbreviated
delirium when I joined in the merriment
… of the ridiculous …of the sublime

Dad farted and told mom to knock it off
or she'd have to sleep in the garage
All of us knew that mom never farted
Not aloud that is – that's when granny lost retention
… pissed herself, and hence, required the attention
of my inculpable mother, since

Mom was the primary slave in those days
not to mention, one might posit
she didn't want anyone fucking around in her linen closet
messing around with her blues and grays

At my young age I couldn't begin to realize the extent
to which those wonderful characters would play
in the (absurd) story of my life

Sort of a Robin Hoodlum

Down at the station, I've got 400 drivers and baggage handlers
Men who respect and listen to my every word as if it was gospel
And then I have you two, who think I'm a dumb son of a bitch
... don't know nothin'!

Dad went into one of his rants that day
a prompt for my brother and his pal, Carl
to subsequently liberate, and then
present dad with two gunny sacks
full of striped range balls
compliments of the Flying Hills Golf Course
a mile and a half from our elevated
backyard of a tee box
and overlooking acres of jackrabbits
and sage, the ideal stage for receiving
a deluge of possibilities – shots
both errant and accurate
that my brother had provided our father
as a show of his appreciation

Dinger

Dad came out of the stands, way too excited and accidentally
tripped me as I rounded 3rd, skinning the underside of my elbow –
an immediate strawberry appeared as I rose to my running feet

I was on THE cloud nine, acting on absolute impulse
It was 83 degrees that night. Crazy bastards in yellow wool outfits
all about my size

Obscure, though somehow, very familiar, awaited me under
the spotlights of baseball heaven – blazing down resplendent
on home plate to mug me in celebration

I was in a total time warp ... eternal. Elsie was in the stands
little doll, sixth grade Elsie. *Lord I want to be a Christian
in 'a my heart ... in 'a my heart.* I love this country!

I love Pee Wee and The Dizz, Joe Garagiola and Tony Kubek!
My dad's buddy from work caught the ball with the front windshield
of his Chevy Wagon — had the appearance of a fried egg

The volunteer ump shook his head and asked me (after the dust
had died), "You know where that pitch was?" I said, "Letter high?"
He said, "It was high alright" His hyperbolic mime of hairy arms

spoke to a vertical fish tale

Half Day Boat, Shelter Island

The Coronado Bridge wouldn't figure
into the San Diego skyline for ten more years
and cigarettes were a quarter a pack when
Mister Moore picked eleven of us up
at the crack of dawn –
a gang of gluey-eyed, gassy-with-junk-food
sons of mostly, unionized democrats
destined for Shelter Island
& the half day boat he'd booked us on

With tackle boxes and rods chaotic in a trunk
a pack of young bloods
some of whom, stunk to the high heavens
with the creek and the river waders, foul
with fetid mud remaining
from our weeks-old, Tijuana River angling
and fish-gut gear
Windows wide open, "Sugar Shack" escaping
a period piece blasting, droning
to the glazed doughnut mouthfuls, munched
and slurped of the thermos coffee …
scalded cheeks and stupid morning tongue

Salty eyes watered dockside early
with the rocking squeal of piers and tires
reeling to the rubbing of the moorings
and the teeter totter wobble of our arrival
in the filmy mist, met there by a pelican dredging
in an open chest for day old bait. Its
tacky, webbed-foot waddle to get away, played back-up
off the creaking planks of creosote timbers

Silver lifeless spills glinted from its bill
like a bucket sluicing., the big bird
slurped by the berth of the boat we'd board

— condensation belched from an old Merc's sputtering idle –
The lilt of its toxic plumes, loomed above us, assailed us
before the sure-footed duo of midnight bar fight brawlers
(half of our sea-scabbing crew) un-clove-hitched us
from the rust-encrusted cleats, freed us
from the vessel's slip — choked us, on the fumes
of ignited gasoline

We set off into the foamy wake of ferries beyond the break
where gulls and lesser terns swarmed our departure
and bilge waters sighed where we'd anchor in the blue-green
Sargasso lagoons of the kelp riatas – elastic red beds
of sea rope lazy on the currents quavering forests
and blooms, where a death grip put a stranglehold
on a tangled, jaundiced jack, & the cocaine-white breast
of a gull-gushing blood, ruby-red-feathered and gaffed-obscene
by the nasty cast of a screw-loose, yahoo teen

I spent the greater part of that day below deck, alternating
from a rocking cradle of a bunk, to puking my guts out
in the vessel's filthy head. One of the crew, at the end of the day
cleaned a bonito for me to take
and Mr. Moore said that the next time they'd bring me along
to outsource the chum tank. I was not amused at the time
as I could only find thanks in the touchdown of unwavering earth —
finally free from the merciless movement of the sea

Day of Darkness

As sophomores, my friend and I
had procured the passes, exclusive chits
excusing us from study hall –
those given strictly to the privileged
athletes being groomed
for intra-mural and district contests
thus, the need for extra time to run 2 plus miles
up to the summit of Mt. Helix & back

We foraged on pomegranates along the way
snaking up the hill and taking
our premeditated detour to the reservoir
— where we'd jump from the rebar rungs of a tower
every graduation measuring a foot, into twelve feet
of its cool, teal depths
I thought it greener than blue
and a bit murky too, though
there was no hint of a brackish scent at all
It was always a refreshing dip on a warm
often humid, So-Cal afternoon

We were cross-country runners — mediocre
to inferior cross country runners, and while
heartthrob of the Italian coach's daughter
Brian Sipe, ran plays with his Foothillers
irrespectively inside and under the gridiron oval
and the Fletcher Hills heat, my buddy and I
would escape the confines of athleticism again
coast back down in physically educated form, lest we
be noticed by one of the less benign athletic directors

Gasping into the locker room stench, *l'odeur
d' aisselle* (from my second year of French) — and of the
essence of gym socks, its leakage of reekage
escaping the banks of the vented compartments

— cells of metal shells for week-old jocks, …assaulted us
prior to entering the communist showers
where we'd lather our backsides down real good and run a bit
to gather momentum — hitting the tiles we'd drop and slide
…the entire span of that steamy bay
And in addition to the welts from the sopped-towel snapping
we'd invariably accrue the chafing of after-burn on our asses
often lasting several days

It was on one of those days, we'd be caught
by a county official at the reservoir. He'd reported us
to the school, and the school, in turn, funneled it back
with a scrap of damnation to our parents. When I got home
ruby stains on my hands and lips; there, on the living room sofa
I found my father sobbing. It was on that darkest of days
in late November of 1963

Ice Cream Bandits

The Ice Cream truck sputtered up and down the tacky asphalt streets
of our neighborhood in the afternoon hours every day
in the summer months. The driver, I'm guessing, in his seventies
was probably supplementing his income of Social Security and a paltry
military retirement check, selling frozen treats back then
He wore an old bomber's jacket... like an ace or a navigator
from the movie *12 O'clock High* or maybe, he'd been a clerk, a typist
who'd pilfered the jacket from a downed air commander's sea bag
after the real pilot, an ace —a hero, died or something, but in any case ...
on he'd jingle (and moo), a cowbell for a car horn

Up and down our streets and avenues in his self-owned, modified
late model, mini-pickup, hauling a large ice chest that sat in the bed
It had several compartments with levers like a real Good Humor rig
but just enough of a knock-off to give off that unofficial demeanor
a signal to us, the adolescent perps responsible for most of the neighborhood
misdemeanors, that would somehow diminish the fear of our temptation
to jump aboard and open the freezer doors, reach into one of those
cold dark stores and pull out a couple of Eskimo Pies — sling them
onto one of the freshly mowed Bermuda or dichondra yards
Surprisingly, we'd have enough composure and focus to direct
our tosses prior to bailing, and retrieve the chocolate, gelid booty. Then we'd
get away down the street, ecstatic, and giddy with the excitement
of doing something so very wrong — almost irreverent

Ice Cream Bandits – that's what we were. Goddamn, we had balls
back then – Not so much anymore. That old fart was just sandbagging us
waiting for that one day when he slammed on the brakes and I ran into
the rear bumper before I could hop aboard. I could've been injured, broke
some teeth or something, but we were rubber-like and resilient
whack-a-mole menaces out there in those streets . I just sort of bounced off
the back of that truck, bruised my shin slightly below the knee. It needed to be
drained for a while so I lied like hell about how I'd done it ... fuck!
Telling the truth was just out of the question

Cathedral Hills

A few years prior to the urethane
skateboard wheel designs
that would surface out of the
sidewalk surfing craze
like the bitch'n candy apple paint jobs
of the Mustangs and the Stingrays

We'd take apart our metal skates
the ones with the key on a string
Nail the metal rollers
to the crudely hewn slabs of Doug Fir
A ripsaw that my dad kept would work
with or against the grain
Any and all projects requiring a saw
back in those days

We'd spray paint these banana boards
splayed across the editorial pages of the UT
Masking-taped them, to a cold garage floor
Model airplane-decaled them, squirted them
with the oil of three in one, for cutting
the ball-bearing sludge, a mixture of
afternoon humidity and the dry valley dust

The first board I made was a Pepto-Bismol pink
had jet black polka dots and was the same
plank I had my accident on…up at Cathedral Hills

Out of boredom for the pendulous motion, I had decided
to challenge myself and abstain from the slalom up there
so I altered by opting to a downhill bearing
resulting in an imperative to bail. This was due
to the intrepid shuddering of increased acceleration
probably fifteen mph, a speed from which I'd leap

and spill off into a spider-legged sprawl
leaving the flesh of my elbows and knees
on the asphalt as I crawled off the street
All the way home, I wailed like a child on fire
looking for a lake to jump into
My mother cried too, "Jesus, honey!"

A bloody mess, she took me into the bathroom
Immersed me in a cold tub of water
and after I'd dried, she applied Mercurochrome
and bandages … what a burn and a bummer!
I gritted my teeth but couldn't stop crying
when my mother poured me a shot of bourbon

— a neat little glass of amber nectar
that had me gasping; and she didn't balk when I
breathlessly asked her … for another measure
to deal with those pulsing, cutaneous embers of pain

Pool Guests

Uninvited, we leapt into the cool-blue, sparkling waters
and out of the hammering heat, a rooftop ooze
of weepy tar-like composition — shingles seeped
the black tacky teardrops that would stick
to the soles of our feet and we'd let out a contagion
of exhilaration, burst into a flurry of raucous cries
under the vast, oppressive umbrella
...of July's sizzling summertime skies

Having neglected to test and add chlorine, none
of us knew what awaited us, didn't know bacteria
would grow — find a home in the pores of our skin
So, suffice it to say, we kept on scaling
the aluminum ladder at the side of the house ...
around and around we'd go

Countless times we'd leap into the cool silk, splooshing!
Luxuriant, blue tiled and with the light-hearts
for its soothing lyrics and marine design, sang the song
of idle filtrations, while the adults, the parents of kids
were off and gone on extended vacation

For the pool below we'd leapt into
Those parents of children would not know
What the parents of children could not prove
When the parents of children were not home

Agnostics all, until the eventual neighborhood outbreak
of folliculitis

Spit Pea Soup

I'd like to recount a family luncheon gathering at our dining room table
where the light poured in from the front of the house. Dad had just hired
an alcoholic to hang wallpaper in that nook (off of the kitchen) a floral design
that gave the room somewhat of an all-season, universal look

We'd convene at this table for every meal that mom would serve
played cards and board games — shooting the breeze
we'd even hit a political nerve in some of our neighbors, friends
or extended family members

A stage was set on one of those days, where an audacious dare
took place. Father, like a pufferfish feigned, with lampoon balloons
for cheeks, …staggered us when he spat a bloated mouthful
of split pea soup into my brother's face

My plucky brother had baited our union man of a sire
to unload the exaggerated mouthful, leaving brother visibly sad
in his Oliver Goldsmith frames – Those enticing every jock
and schoolyard bully, to isolate him, a horn-rimmed dupe
for the numerous, and cruel, four-eyed monikers he'd weather

The unpleasant consequence of this challenge, an adherent coat
phlegm-like in consistency, dripped with the slow motion viscosity
into an expression of disbelief – the result of my brother's ignorant taunt
that no one at the table, had initially thought of as a spectacle
even slightly humorous

Not until the shock would erode, could the complexity for amusement
be completely perceived

On the Cusp of the Hep Cats and the Hippies

The door bell sounded at the welcome mat. Out front
a squad car held my brother in a shock of handcuffs

I could see him in the window through an obscurity
of rain – grey sheets on a bias in the washed-out dusk

He'd taken a five finger discount — the officer at the door
announced; lifted two tins of spendy, Spanish octopi

nigh and neon the hissing, of an uptown Safeway, another
dark wet Saturday night of espresso and mollusk sharing

at El Cajon Blvd's, Upper Cellar, a beatnik dive, a West Coast
mid century thriving nighttime nightclub, that came alive &

where its marquee would strobe on wet evenings and stretch
reflections of rain across the pavement. Inside, guitars

and harmonicas jammed; probed the soft, folky, tobacco haze
Outside, aspiring (dead)beats discreetly liver-lipped the sticks

of *mota* from *Michoacán* in an alleyway of a place my brother
could rehearse his cool; a university coffee house, where during breaks

Blues and Haikus played backup to the din of pseudo-
intellectualizing, existential bohemianizing, in a decade where the lid

was about to blow off of the status quo — where my pasty white brother
a lower middle class kid from the burbs, sat on his hat in the rain

a stupid flattened beret, required of rendering an impression
— of one hincty Parisian poet's disdain

Conquering Cock Rock

The boys who'd founded the clubs, who'd come up with
the elaborate initiations entailing feats of strength and courage
were the little sons of bitches who'd excused themselves
from participation — those whose folly it was, as architects of these
intimate cadres and organizations, fly by night in nature
needn't perform

Integral to these challenges was a hierarchy, typically led
by two older, smartass, malicious adolescent monsters
They had the hideous reputations for cruelty and tireless ridicule
Often targeting the misfortunate traits of the special education
children at school

So with certainty it can be said, they were exempt from sharing
in their own inventions of valor, some of which, included
prospective members to queue-up against a shed
or the trundling paneled doors, before the two-car garages
facing-off with a firing squad of bb rifles, most prevalent
throughout our neighborhood

The air-pumped shots were a pell-mell — a hapless grouping
of ass welts extruding, yet appeared like the angry hives
that mothers would treat, unwise to its origin
of sadistic design, with a corticosteroid or an antihistamine

Jack from Sunny Slopes and I, in our naked feet ran
8 miles of asphalt pledging one of these gangs – returned
on sore soles puckering with dense blue bladders
plump with blood on the pads of our feet. Our parents and doctors
intervened with a wealth of prudence, I mean, I would gingerly walk
on crutches for a couple of weeks

Other tasks that held comparable risks included bounding from
dangerous rock to dangerous rock, inching with peristaltic torsos
into the crevices of the gargantuan granite monoliths — slabs
and shelves under which, rattlers, scorpions and tarantulas too
undoubtedly found relief in the shade of the cool, dark earth
and out of the bake of that hot inland sun

... but there was no relief from the litany of taunts
or the din of a ribbing that another potential inductee would endure
squawked-at and scorned, while his final challenge stood erect
before him, ... the impossible-to-scale, face of that phallic, igneous dome
where many a petroglyphic-pornographer found his filthy little mind a home

We wouldn't have believed that an eleven year old could run up that rock
if we hadn't seen it

Resigning Myself to the Dotted Line

"The only true currency in this bankrupt world is what you share with someone else while you're uncool." — Lester Bangs

I'd gone mad – as mad as a teen could go
Me and the old man, suffering through
a contemptible relationship when I shaved
my head and he struck me – an open hand
that felt like a clenched fist. Then he kicked me
in the coccyx for the ugly shape of my skull
So ugly, my mother would weep – just eighteen
& thought I'd arrived, so I threatened to leave

I'd join the Marines. But first I'd drink
those quarts of beer, those I'd assumed would
further stimulate my already keen perception
of being – Teetering, intoxicated — teenagers
raging with dreams atop our favorite drinking spot
a mesa, looking out on the El Cajon, Friday night sparkle
of sprawling lights

So completely ripped and altered, and riding a righteous
buzz, we bolted down, my held-back buddy and I
down to the bottom of "The Box," where we blasphemed
our way into the Hi Ho Club on Fletcher Pkwy –
Courageous and emboldened moreover, coming-on
to these girls, who were the same girls we were incapable
of approaching sober. It was a wild time for trying on our cool
our hipsters, ever-looking to score after school

It was a complete morph from my presumably normal
behavior – Jesus back then, my Lord, my Savior
ever-battling the natural inclinations, juvenile gyrations
that would jinx me when I would finally sign those papers
& enlist in *The Corps*. Six months later, I'd piss myself
on the banks of the Perfume River

Truant Officer

Jerry Jung was one of those guys
who gave off a real familial vibe
I would never have thought he'd snub me –
Screw me, and a brother
this guy with a genuine smile

Our liberations often occurred
via the choir window
Jerry sang bass. I was a baritone
We were a gleeful duo, often
ignoring our responsibility for vocal symbiosis
escaping the institutional confines
many a day to sit in the sand, dream together
about what we'd do down the road
post-grad. We couldn't bear another hosanna

Jerry fucking Jung and me
tried out for the varsity baseball team
Neither of us would make the cut
and after which, we lost touch
until I saw him again at the induction center
in August—the summer of '67
where and when we had our hooves
and assholes probed; pledged
to keep our country safe from the commies
or some such …
Jerry joined the Army
and for the sake of a perfectly sonorous segue
I joined the Marines

I'd run into him again around three-thirty
a.m., and three years later, on Highway 80
It was in the proximity
of our old elementary school on Johnson Avenue
a benign institution where we'd shared

some unruly laughs — but lest I deviate
I was asleep in the back seat
of a '66 Falcon that my roommate, Dutch
possessed and was slightly drunk driving, returning
from El Toro Marine Corps Base
and a party that some old jarheads
had thrown me, ... when *protégé*
Officer Jerry fucking Jung and his Don Ameche
lookalike-of-a-mentor pulled us over in a cruiser
I think they were looking to kill some time before
Winchell's on the boulevard opened its doors

In any case, Jung wouldn't give this long-haired palomine
and one time juvenile cut-up classmate of ours, a break
even though we'd all grown up together, all of us Salk subjects
queuing up together in the gymnasium, big players
in the cafeteria food fights, and all of us privy to the female
reproduction videos as 5th grade AV monitors; we three —
sitting on one of those ubiquitous yellow Laidlaw transports
flipping the bird and farting, laughing about the stupidest shit
like the time ...

Our maladjusted buddy, Dutch, a real class clown
retrieved a dead dove that had been struck
by an early morning delivery truck. He brought the coo-less
bird into the schoolyard and chased some of the girls with it
shaking its lifeless form at them. In class he removed it from
his Porky The Pig and Pals lunch box, chucked the deceased bird
with a broken neck, slamming it against the blackboard
we guessed, foremost for its startling effect — but it would
also serve as a show of courage and grow him a lot of laughs

The down of dove, like snowflakes, lightly landed
on our classroom floor, and the sound of our
substitute teacher's creaking shoes, squealed

like worn brake pads when he turned abruptly
It was all in synch with the piece of chalk
in the elderly man's hand — a caterwaul across the slate
to work out something questionably educational
Unfortunately, Dutch had the nostrils that would flare
when he would fuck with you, an unintentional
tell to his catalog of incessant culpabilities
— a trait that, in concert with one of the girls ratting-him-out
would invariably get him busted

But in the wee morning hours of our lost world's rotation
in 1970, when the length of my hair was just beginning to set me apart
from the squares, still smarting from my time in the Corps
and a tour in Southeast Asia, Dutch would be taken
– hauled off to the hoosegow with his fingers turning
a bruisy blue and numbly tingling – the blood supply reduced
by the shackles cinched so tightly, with such cruelty
around his wrists, they'd score. The same kid who'd
put a fun-loving Jung in stitches, a mere decade or so before

…Officer Jung, it would seem, was an obvious rookie, acted
as if he didn't know that I was the kid with whom…he'd shared
his carefree dreams, climbed out of the choir window on those
many days we'd played hooky

Not the sort of loyalty Dutch and I would've expected from an old
classmate, a chum we'd grown to love back then…and I'd be damned
when Jung glossed over both of our I.D.s…and couldn't even muster
a flipping grin

Afterthoughts —

Finally, for my Tobias Wolff moment. Just as I have written pieces presenting sort of a hybrid of poetry and prose, I have likewise created a fusion of dead-on depictions and fiction. I'd just like to say as a bit of a disclaimer, that although every individual piece in this book has a specific factual foundation, the inaccurate blending of characters and incidents, as I imagined them from that far off place in time, has occurred. At my age, who remembers the past as it actually happened? In "Ice Cream Bandits," as an example, having sent a preview to my recently-turned septuagenarian friend living in England, remembering him as my partner in crime, hopping like hobos aboard the rear end of a *moosical*, cowbell clanging, ice cream truck; stealing Eskimo Pies and Push-ups from a freezer box. He had no memory of those frozen thefts so I reckon it was another rascal I'd hung with. It's just not something one would forget, unless he was not a party to it, or he'd undergone a lobotomy.

Other embellishments were less accidental and were created in a more self-indulgent vein, e.g., " 'Twas a Mitzvah," and "El Cajon Valley." Yes, my aunt and I used to grind against each other and it was stimulating, but I totally amped-it-up with some delicious hyperbole, because I was having so much fun with it. And, as for keeping two sets of plates, one for dairy and one for meat …hell, my parents weren't practicing Jews — I hadn't been bar mitzvahed, and never recognized Passover or any of the other High Holidays, until my introduction to Judaism, years later, when I married a Ukrainian Jew. In 1991, when NBC decided to renew *Seinfeld*, I would seriously consider converting from atheism.

My grandfather was ex-law enforcement in some capacity, I think in Kansas City, MO. He would drop-in on us from time to time, along with his second wife, and their daughter, my aunt, who was two years older than me. They kept a kosher household in L. A. — wouldn't have been caught dead having a burger and a shake (together). And although, I'd lead a reader to believe otherwise, I was raised in the Southern Baptist style of religiosity, my dog tags later declaring me a Presbyterian, the image of the *glove compartment revolver* was not a bullshit image I invented.

All that being said, I was especially careful not to have identified children or adults by their actual names. In both, "*Brownie*" and "Truant Officer," the names have been altered, but the characters depicted are precisely who I remember them to be.

While putting this collection together, it came to me that the writings I'd included were but a few in a tome of shenanigans and capers we'd pulled off as kids. And as I thought back, I realized how fortunate we were to have the love and understanding of parents who'd remembered themselves as children, too. Believe you me, they had some stories of their own. And on a final note — I took Spanish in high school, not French. I said I took French because it rhymed with stench in "Day of Darkness."

That's about it.
Fred

About the Author

Fred Rosenblum is a 'Left Coast' poet, residing in San Diego with his wife of 46 years. He is the author of two previous collections of poetry (*Hollow Tin Jingles* and *Vietnumb*) and has appeared in a variety of publications throughout the US and Canada since 2009 — most notably, *Consequence Magazine, Cirque Journal*, and the *Aurorean*.

Fomite

About Fomite

A fomite is a medium capable of transmitting infectious organisms from one individual to another.

"The activity of art is based on the capacity of people to be infected by the feelings of others." Tolstoy, *What Is Art?*

Writing a review on Amazon, Good Reads, Shelfari, Library Thing or other social media sites for readers will help the progress of independent publishing. To submit a review, go to the book page on any of the sites and follow the links for reviews. Books from independent presses rely on reader to reader communications.

For more information or to order any of our books, visit
http://www.fomitepress.com/FOMITE/Our_Books.html

More Titles from Fomite...

Novels
Joshua Amses — *During This, Our Nadir*
Joshua Amses — *Ghatsr*
Joshua Amses — *Raven or Crow*
Joshua Amses — *The Moment Before an Injury*
Jaysinh Birjepatel — *Nothing Beside Remains*
Jaysinh Birjepatel — *The Good Muslim of Jackson Heights*
David Brizer — *Victor Rand*
Paula Closson Buck — *Summer on the Cold War Planet*
Dan Chodorkoff — *Loisaida*
David Adams Cleveland — *Time's Betrayal*
Jaimee Wriston Colbert — *Vanishing Acts*
Roger Coleman — *Skywreck Afternoons*
Marc Estrin — *Hyde*
Marc Estrin — *Kafka's Roach*
Marc Estrin — *Speckled Vanities*
Zdravka Evtimova — *In the Town of Joy and Peace*
Zdravka Evtimova — *Sinfonia Bulgarica*
Zdravka Evtimova — *You Can Smile on Wednesdays*
Peter Fortunato — *Carnevale*
Daniel Forbes — *Derail This Train Wreck*
Greg Guma — *Dons of Time*
Richard Hawley — *The Three Lives of Jonathan Force*
Lamar Herrin — *Father Figure*
Michael Horner — *Damage Control*
Ron Jacobs — *All the Sinners Saints*
Ron Jacobs — *Short Order Frame Up*
Ron Jacobs — *The Co-conspirator's Tale*
Scott Archer Jones — *And Throw Away the Skins*
Scott Archer Jones — *A Rising Tide of People Swept Away*

Fomite

Julie Justicz — *Degrees of Difficulty*
Maggie Kast — *A Free Unsullied Land*
Darrell Kastin — *Shadowboxing with Bukowski*
Coleen Kearon — *#triggerwarning*
Coleen Kearon — *Feminist on Fire*
Jan English Leary — *Thicker Than Blood*
Diane Lefer — *Confessions of a Carnivore*
Rob Lenihan — *Born Speaking Lies*
Douglas Milliken — *Our Shadow's Voice*
Colin Mitchell — *Roadman*
Ilan Mochari — *Zinsky the Obscure*
Peter Nash — *Parsimony*
Peter Nash — *The Perfection of Things*
George Ovitt — *Stillpoint*
George Ovitt — *Tribunal*
Gregory Papadoyiannis — *The Baby Jazz*
Pelham — *The Walking Poor*
Andy Potok — *My Father's Keeper*
Frederick Ramey — *Comes A Time*
Joseph Rathgeber — *Mixedbloods*
Kathryn Roberts — *Companion Plants*
Robert Rosenberg — *Isles of the Blind*
Fred Russell — *Rafi's World*
Ron Savage — *Voyeur in Tangier*
David Schein — *The Adoption*
Lynn Sloan — *Principles of Navigation*
L.E. Smith — *The Consequence of Gesture*
L.E. Smith — *Travers' Inferno*
L.E. Smith — *Untimely RIPped*
Bob Sommer — *A Great Fullness*
Tom Walker — *A Day in the Life*
Susan V. Weiss — *My God, What Have We Done?*
Peter M. Wheelwright — *As It Is On Earth*
Suzie Wizowaty — *The Return of Jason Green*

Poetry
Anna Blackmer — *Hexagrams*
Antonello Borra — *Alfabestiario*
Antonello Borra — *AlphaBetaBestiaro*
Antonello Borra — *Fabbrica delle idee/The Factory of Ideas*
L. Brown — *Loopholes*
Sue D. Burton — *Little Steel*
David Cavanagh — *Cycling in Plato's Cave*
James Connolly — *Picking Up the Bodies*
Greg Delanty — *Loosestrife*
Mason Drukman — *Drawing on Life*
J. C. Ellefson — *Foreign Tales of Exemplum and Woe*
Tina Escaja/Mark Eisner — *Caida Libre/Free Fall*
Anna Faktorovich — *Improvisational Arguments*

Fomite

Barry Goldensohn — *Snake in the Spine, Wolf in the Heart*
Barry Goldensohn — *The Hundred Yard Dash Man*
Barry Goldensohn — *The Listener Aspires to the Condition of Music*
R. L. Green — *When You Remember Deir Yassin*
Gail Holst-Warhaft — *Lucky Country*
Raymond Luczak — *A Babble of Objects*
Kate Magill — *Roadworthy Creature, Roadworthy Craft*
Tony Magistrale — *Entanglements*
Gary Mesick — *General Discharge*
Andreas Nolte — *Mascha: The Poems of Mascha Kaléko*
Sherry Olson — *Four-Way Stop*
Brett Ortler — *Lessons of the Dead*
Aristea Papalexandrou/Philip Ramp — *Μας προσπερνά/It's Overtaking Us*
Janice Miller Potter — *Meanwell*
Janice Miller Potter — *Thoreau's Umbrella*
Philip Ramp — *The Melancholy of a Life as the Joy of Living It Slowly Chills*
Joseph D. Reich — *A Case Study of Werewolves*
Joseph D. Reich — *Connecting the Dots to Shangrila*
Joseph D. Reich — *The Derivation of Cowboys and Indians*
Joseph D. Reich — *The Hole That Runs Through Utopia*
Joseph D. Reich — *The Housing Market*
Kenneth Rosen and Richard Wilson — *Gomorrah*
Fred Rosenblum — *Vietnumb*
Fred Rosenblum — *Playing Chicken with an Iron Horse*
David Schein — *My Murder and Other Local News*
Harold Schweizer — *Miriam's Book*
Scott T. Starbuck — *Carbonfish Blues*
Scott T. Starbuck — *Hawk on Wire*
Scott T. Starbuck — *Industrial Oz*
Seth Steinzor — *Among the Lost*
Seth Steinzor — *To Join the Lost*
Susan Thomas — *In the Sadness Museum*
Susan Thomas — *The Empty Notebook Interrogates Itself*
Paolo Valesio/Todd Portnowitz — *La Mezzanotte di Spoleto/Midnight in Spoleto*
Sharon Webster — *Everyone Lives Here*
Tony Whedon — *The Tres Riches Heures*
Tony Whedon — *The Falkland Quartet*
Claire Zoghb — *Dispatches from Everest*

Stories
MaryEllen Beveridge — *After the Hunger*
MaryEllen Beveridge — *Permeable Boundaries*
Jay Boyer — *Flight*
L. M Brown — *Treading the Uneven Road*
Michael Cocchiarale — *Here Is Ware*
Michael Cocchiarale — *Still Time*
Neil Connelly — *In the Wake of Our Vows*
Catherine Zobal Dent — *Unfinished Stories of Girls*
Zdravka Evtimova — *Carts and Other Stories*

Fomite

John Michael Flynn — *Off to the Next Wherever*
Derek Furr — *Semitones*
Derek Furr — *Suite for Three Voices*
Elizabeth Genovise — *Where There Are Two or More*
Andrei Guriuanu — *Body of Work*
Zeke Jarvis — *In A Family Way*
Arya Jenkins — *Blue Songs in an Open Key*
Jan English Leary — *Skating on the Vertical*
Marjorie Maddox — *What She Was Saying*
William Marquess — *Boom-shacka-lacka*
Gary Miller — *Museum of the Americas*
Jennifer Anne Moses — *Visiting Hours*
Martin Ott — *Interrogations*
Christopher Peterson — *Amoebic Simulacra*
Jack Pulaski — *Love's Labours*
Charles Rafferty — *Saturday Night at Magellan's*
Ron Savage — *What We Do For Love*
Fred Skolnik — *Americans and Other Stories*
Lynn Sloan — *This Far Is Not Far Enough*
L.E. Smith — *Views Cost Extra*
Caitlin Hamilton Summie — *To Lay To Rest Our Ghosts*
Susan Thomas — *Among Angelic Orders*
Tom Walker — *Signed Confessions*
Silas Dent Zobal — *The Inconvenience of the Wings*

Odd Birds
William Benton — *Eye Contact: Writing on Art*
Micheal Breiner — *the way none of this happened*
J. C. Ellefson — *Under the Influence: Shouting Out to Walt*
David Ross Gunn — *Cautionary Chronicles*
Andrei Guriuanu and Teknari — *The Darkest City*
Gail Holst-Warhaft — *The Fall of Athens*
Roger Lebovitz — *A Guide to the Western Slopes and the Outlying Area*
Roger Lebovitz — *Twenty-two Instructions for Near Survival*
dug Nap — *Artsy Fartsy*
Delia Bell Robinson — *A Shirtwaist Story*
Peter Schumann — *Belligerent & Not So Belligerent Slogans from the Possibilitarian Arsenal*
Peter Schumann — *Bread & Sentences*
Peter Schumann — *Children's Deprimer*
Peter Schumann — *Charlotte Salomon*
Peter Schumann — *Diagonal Man Theory + Praxis, Volumes One and Two*
Peter Schumann — *Faust 3*
Peter Schumann — *Planet Kasper, Volumes One and Two*
Peter Schumann — *We*

Plays
Stephen Goldberg — *Screwed and Other Plays*
Michele Markarian — *Unborn Children of America*

Fomite

Essays
Robert Sommer — *Losing Francis: Essays on the Wars at Home*

www.ingramcontent.com/pod-product-compliance
Lightning Source LLC
Chambersburg PA
CBHW030100100526
44591CB00008B/212